You Are a Social Detective!

Explaining Social Thinking to Kids

2nd Edition · Revised and Expanded

Michelle Garcia Winner and **Pamela Crooke**

Illustrations by **Jeff Ebbler**

25+ YRS Social Thinking jr.

Think Social Publishing, Inc., Santa Clara, California
www.socialthinking.com

You Are a Social Detective! Explaining Social Thinking to Kids, 2nd Edition

Michelle Garcia Winner, Pamela Crooke

ISBN: 978-1-936943-55-5 (print)
ISBN: 978-1-936943-53-1 (ebook)

Think Social Publishing, Inc.
404 Saratoga Avenue, Suite 200
Santa Clara, CA 95050
Tel: (408) 557-8595
Fax: (408) 557-8594

Illustrations by Jeff Ebbeler

This book was printed and bound in the United States by Mighty Color Printing.
TSP is a sole source provider of Social Thinking products in the U.S.
Books may be purchased online at www.socialthinking.com

Recommended Teaching & Learning Pathway

for using the Superflex series and the *Superflex Curriculum*

3-Step Pathway for kids ages 5-10*

1 Use Social Detective first to introduce key Social Thinking concepts/Vocabulary to build social awareness.

2 After building social awareness and a social vocabulary, depending on the age of your student, introduce Superflex to teach strategies for self-regulation in a superhero-themed format.

3 Use Brain Eater (or any other Superflex storybooks or games) AFTER teaching the Superflex Curriculum to take learning to a deeper level.

If you're working with kids ages 9-12

Social Thinking and Me is used BEFORE or alongside teaching the *Superflex Curriculum*. This two-book set helps deepen students' understanding of core Social Thinking concepts and gives them lots of practice to build stronger social competencies.

Use the Thinkable storybooks as companions to Unthinkable storybooks. Great tool for focusing on the positive powers in each of our brains.

*Some younger kids with social learning differences may need more time building their Social Detective skills. Wait to start Superflex with them until around age 8.

Find articles and On Demand courses about teaching Superflex plus other books and teaching materials at
www.SocialThinking.com

Get your kids ready for the Superflex Academy with the all-new edition of this award-winning storybook!

Students will ...

- Learn formulas for gathering clues by observing a situation, the people, and what's happening
- Learn to identify feelings and emotions and connect them to behaviors
- Be empowered to figure out how the social world works through their own detective lens
- Understand that all feelings are okay, even uncomfortable ones, and we can still learn and grow
- Get support from emojis and special word banks
- Find Social Thinking® core vocabulary words highlighted throughout to reinforce key learning concepts
- Have numerous opportunities to make smart guesses about various situations
- See examples and tips for school, home, and community life

Dedicated to the many Social Detectives
we've known over the years and our fabulous team of professional,
parent, teen, and kid reviewers, including the Magical Bridge Kindness
Ambassadors, who gave constructive, supportive, and honest
feedback: Adrien, Ana, Anoushka, Bob, David, Grace, Katrina,
Kelvin, Keina, Kristine, Philip, Thomas, and Vivian.
This is a better book because of your input!

Dear Parent and Professional,

While we specifically teach children academics at school, and at home we teach safety and life skills such as crossing a street or making a sandwich, we tend to be quite vague when teaching children what it means to "be social" and relate more effectively with others. Most adults assume children's social brains absorb this type of learning in the moment, largely by watching others. In most cases,  it's assumed that concrete lessons about things like how to say "hi" or how to be part of a group aren't needed. However, the social emotional learning process is the foundation of how we share space together. It is the groundwork of interactive play, working in groups, interpreting literature, following story lines or characters' motivations, hanging out with friends, and understanding the actions and reactions of ourselves and others. It deserves attention—a LOT of attention!

Through the Social Thinking® Methodology we seek to teach implied, hidden, embedded, generally expected but seldom taught social emotional information in a more explicit way, with the goal of increasing our children's **social competencies**. Social competency is much broader than teaching children "social skills." Skills are our behaviors: what we do or say (or don't do or don't say) in a social situation based on who is around. Social competencies encompasses all the thinking and interpretation that happens in our brains before we exhibit a behavior. For example, we might learn to direct our social attention to observe others (and ourselves), draw on the social knowledge we possess about people and situations, interpret what it all means, and then put all this together to figure out (problem solve) how to respond in a way that meets our social goals, no matter what situation we find ourselves in.

In the Social Thinking Methodology we teach social competencies through a core four-step teaching and social learning process: attend, interpret, problem solve, and respond. (Get the full picture in our free article, Social Thinking–Social Competency Model or check out our On Demand modules on this topic at our website, www.socialthinking.com.) *You Are a Social Detective!* teaches children about the first two steps, social attention and interpretation, and acts as a springboard to help them learn to later problem solve and respond. In this book we introduce multiple Social Thinking Vocabulary concepts that, when combined together, begin to build our children's understanding that no matter where we are, we each experience a social emotional chain reaction made up of our thoughts, feelings, behaviors and reactions.

How to Use this Book to Its Fullest

Throughout the book you will see words highlighted in **bold lettering**. These are the key Social Thinking Vocabulary words to teach and emphasize. They are defined in the glossary starting on page xi.

***You Are a Social Detective* is *not* a book that teaches children about behavior change,** although changes in behavior may occur as a result of the teaching. We strongly discourage adults from using this book, or any materials from the Social Thinking Methodology, to teach children that people have any sort of negative thoughts and feelings about their behaviors as a means to punish or shame the child into changing their behaviors. Our goal throughout this book is to promote stronger social attention to key information to allow for social processing and interpretation. In other words, we hope to facilitate a mindset in your teaching that places emphasis on thinking rather than behavior change.

This may be a new perspective for you in teaching social skills to children. If so, please take the time to adjust your own thinking around this before teaching this book to others. There are many free articles about the Social Thinking Methodology on our website, www.socialthinking.com. If you are a parent, educator, or clinician new to Social Thinking, in addition to our articles we offer several "core" books on the methodology (*Why Teach Social Thinking?*, *Social Thinking and Me, and Thinking About YOU Thinking About ME*), alongside On Demand courses and free webinars that introduce you

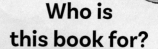

Who is this book for?

- Neurotypical or Neurodivergent children grades K-5

- Children with social learning differences in primary school grades* who have solid to strong language and academic learning abilities

- Children who can begin to imagine what others may be thinking and/or feeling in a situation (emerging perspective taking skills)

* Social learning is slow and deep; these children may need more time exploring and learning the concepts.

to the evidence-based foundation upon which the Social Thinking Methodology is built. These materials accentuate the value in teaching social competencies rather than "social skills" and can help you appreciate this mental shift in how we are teaching the social learning process to children.

What About Superflex? Can't I Start There?

Kids love our Superflex® superhero curriculum! Since its introduction in 2008, children around the globe have learned to recognize the ever-so-clever team of UnthinkaBot (new in 2022) or Unthinkable characters who represent thoughts and actions that can wreak havoc in all of our lives, and learn to use our superflexible thinking strategies to manage them.

But we hit a snag along the way. We discovered that many well-meaning adults were jumping right into teaching the Superflex curriculum, without priming their students' brains to be expert social observers first via the core teachings in *You Are a Social Detective*. That's kind of like expecting kids to learn to make a soufflé without teaching them to first follow a recipe or learn about basic ingredients.

And this is precisely why we don't jump right into teaching the Superflex curriculum before we work (diligently) with students on the core concepts we teach in *Social Detective* (and *Social Thinking and Me*, if you're working with kids a little older). In *Social Detective* we are laying the groundwork in refining social attention to open up children's awareness to the different kinds of smarts we all possess, to what's happening around them (the situation), who the people are in the situation, and then teaching them that every situation comes with certain social expectations (hidden rules) that people don't typically talk about but that affect how people interact together. We do all this first, and THEN we can graduate our students into becoming more aware of their own behaviors and how to successfully self-regulate when around others, as taught in *Superflex*®...*A Superhero Social Thinking*® *Curriculum*.

In the Social Thinking Social Competency Model, we describe learning these first two important core concepts as learning to "Attend," (observe) and "Interpret," (figure out the situation and what is happening). Once you understand those, you can then learn how to "Problem Solve" and "Respond."

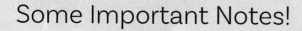

Some Important Notes!

We recommend that parents/caregivers and professionals first read *You Are a Social Detective!* by themselves to learn our unique and explicit Social Thinking® Vocabulary. Once everyone learns the vocabulary, it can be used during teachable moments everywhere: in class, on the playground, in the community, and at home as needed. We then recommend reading this book with kids in sections and combining that reading with real-life discussions about how the concepts apply to them personally.

REVIEW the vocabulary before teaching it! We suggest you break down the content as follows:

1. My Smarts, School Smarts, Social Smarts, pages 1-7
2. The Situation, pages 8-11
3. Being a Social Detective, pages 12-17
4. Smart Guess, pages 18-23
5. Hidden Rules in a Situation, Expected Behaviors, pages 24-37
6. Unexpected Behaviors, pages 38-45
7. Review and Practice, pages 46-53

Talking about Confused Thoughts and Feelings

As we mentioned previously, this book is not about getting children to change their behavior. We're here to encourage children to learn new ways to think about themselves in relation to others, and yes, that process will inevitably involve talking about behavior. But we want you to do this in a different way. A Social Thinking way.

Please review the concept **confused thoughts and feelings** in the vocabulary definitions that follow before introducing and using this concept with your child/student. It is important we first teach individuals to notice the thoughts and feelings (both good/okay and confused) they have about what *others* say and do. Explore the social expectations they hold about how other people act. This is a crucial first step in their learning to self-reflect. We want that discussion to occur before we ask our kids to consider that others have these same social expectations, as well as okay (or good or neutral) and confused thoughts and feelings about what they do and say (their behaviors). We *strongly discourage* adults to use this, or any Social Thinking materials, to teach children that people have negative thoughts and feelings about their behaviors with the hope of getting them to change their behaviors. That's not the Social Thinking way!

And, before we wrap up, one more thing: always put the attention on children's behavior, not on the children themselves. So when we're talking about expected or unexpected behaviors for the situation, or about confused thoughts or feelings, we talk about this in relation to what a child is saying or doing, not as a statement about the child. Please try to notice whether or not, or to what extent you may be saying things like, "When you touch other people's stuff, others have confused thoughts *about you*." Keep the focus on the behavior and not on the child. For example, if a child grabs another child's backpack, you might say, "I noticed you grabbed her backpack without permission. That made me have confused thoughts and feelings about why you touched her stuff. Next time you should ask her if it's okay." The goal is never to shame or blame kids: it's to teach them to think about how others view their behaviors—what they're saying or doing—and give them strategies for turning the situation around to be more positive for all.

This isn't just a book for kids ...

Our hope is that *You Are a Social Detective!* will be used as a way to introduce Social Thinking concepts to general education teachers, paraprofessionals, parents, caregivers, special educators, grandparents, siblings, day-care workers, scout leaders, etc., and of course, to those kids who are learning to be Social Detectives!

Be sure to use the vocabulary everywhere! With a little thought you'll notice countless places and situations to reinforce the vocabulary your children are learning. Enjoy watching your students and kids blossom into Social Detectives!

Social Thinking® Vocabulary

Note to parents and teachers:
The following vocabulary concepts are part of a larger Social Thinking Methodology that has many components to help us all talk about social information and expectations more clearly. The vocabulary in this book can be used all day, everyday, with children and students to help them build stronger social awareness and understanding.

Body in the Group: Your body is in the group if others see and feel you are part of the group. For example, when you are standing, this means keeping your body about one arm's length away from others. Your head and the front of your body will be turned toward others in the group.

Body out of the Group: This is the opposite of Body in the Group. Your body is out of the group if others see and feel you are not part of the group. You may be standing or sitting apart from others, or your head and body are turned away from others. This sends a nonverbal signal that you are not interested in being with the group. Sometimes it's okay or required to move your body out of the group.

Brain in the Group: Your brain is in the group when others think and feel you are paying attention to what is happening in the group. You keep your brain in the group by thinking about others with your eyes and listening to what they are talking about.

Brain out of the Group: This is the opposite of Brain in the Group. Your brain is out of the group when you are not paying attention to what others are saying or doing. Your brain can be out of the group while your body is still in the group!

For more information on the Social Thinking Vocabulary, visit www.socialthinking.com.

Confused Thoughts and Feelings: We have thoughts about what the people around us are doing or saying, and they have thoughts about what we are doing or saying. When a person has a confused thought about what we do or say, it means we did some unexpected behavior that made that person take notice and feel confused, upset, or frustrated. In a similar way, we take notice of other people's behaviors that make us have confused thoughts and feelings about what they are saying or doing.

SPECIAL NOTE ON THIS TERM: *When working with students on this concept, it is ineffective teaching to simply tell them that others have confused thoughts. Instead, adults should use this concept to teach our students about the social emotional chain reaction. This helps them connect thoughts to feelings and behaviors, so they notice how they form "okay/good thoughts" and "confused thoughts" about others' behaviors, and how this thought turns into a not-so-great feeling, which impacts how they treat that person!*

Expected Behaviors for the Situation: These are things people do and say that may result in others having okay/good or neutral thoughts about these words or actions. People usually feel okay or neutral or calm around others who show expected behaviors. Doing what is **expected** is different based on the situation: where we are and who we are with. Expected behaviors are the hidden rules in a situation.

Hidden Rules: These are the rules that tell us what to do in situations. People don't usually talk about them, but we are expected to know and follow them. The Hidden Rules are expected behaviors.

Okay/good (or neutral) Thoughts and Feelings: Others have thoughts about what we do or say, and we have thoughts about what others do or say. When a person has an okay/good thought (or neutral thought) about what we do or say, it means we figured out what behaviors are expected in that situation and with that person. When others have okay/good (or neutral) thoughts about what we do or say, they feel good and will remember how they felt. We also remember the good thoughts we have about other people's behavior or what they said or did. This makes us feel good about being around them.

School Smarts: Different types of "smarts" in our brains that we use for school learning: math smarts, computer smarts, music smarts, science smarts, and many more.

Situation: The "situation" refers to where we are, who we are with, and what is happening. A setting, such as a classroom, can have many different situations in it. For instance, storytime is a situation, silent work is a situation, and listening to the teacher talk is a situation.

Smart Guess: This is when we use all of our tools (remembering, seeing, hearing, knowing, and feeling) to figure out a situation and then make a guess based on what we know about the world. Teachers also expect us to make smart guesses in class. Once they teach us information we are supposed to be able to use that information to guess what else might be needed or what might happen. Smart guesses are "expected behaviors" and may result in others having okay/good (or neutral) thoughts because they know we are trying to figure things out!

Social Detective: Every one of us is a Social Detective. We are Social Detectives when we use our Social Detective tools—our eyes, ears, brains and hearts—to figure out a situation, who is around, and what they might be thinking or planning to do next or are presently doing. Being a Social Detective also helps us figure out what people mean by what they say and do.

Social Detective Tools: We all have Social Detective tools that we can use anytime to help us figure out people and places. These super important tools are our eyes, ears, and brain and, of course, understanding the feelings of others (sometimes people use a picture of a heart to represent that people have feelings).

Social Emotional Chain Reaction: Our thoughts, feelings, actions, and reactions are all connected and form a chain reaction. Someone does or says something, and we have a thought about it. We also have a feeling about it. If it's an okay/good thought, we probably have a good feeling. Our thoughts and feelings connect to our actions, and our actions (behaviors) create a new thought (and feeling) in others. Others have a reaction to us as a result and the chain reaction starts all over again.

Social Smarts: This is the type of "smarts" in our brains that we use **whenever we are around other people**. Social smarts help our brains know that others are having thoughts about what we do or say, and we are having thoughts about what they do or say whenever we are together. We use social smarts in school, at home, and EVERYWHERE!

Social Thinker: Each of us is a "social thinker" every day, each time we are around other people. It means we are aware that people are around us and having thoughts about our behaviors and that we are doing the same toward them. We are social thinkers even when people are not talking to or playing with us. Social thinkers know that when we are in a classroom, we often share the same or a similar thought when the teacher is teaching. Learning to become a better social thinker is what we all do throughout our lives!

Thinking with Your Eyes: This means you are using your eyes to show your brain is thinking about other people and thinking about what they may be thinking and feeling. This makes them feel that you are paying attention and are interested in them, which makes them feel okay/good.

Unexpected Behaviors for the Situation: These are things people do and say that may result in confused thoughts about the behavior. Unexpected behaviors can make others feel really confused. Doing what is **unexpected** is different based on the situation: where we are, who we are with, and what's happening.

Wacky Guess: This is when we don't have enough information to make a guess or we forget or just don't use our tools (remembering, seeing, hearing, knowing, and feeling) to figure things out. Instead we may make a random guess or make a guess based on our own thoughts and interests, without connecting to the facts. Wacky guesses are usually "unexpected" and usually result in confused thoughts. Teachers do not expect us to make wacky guesses in class or with our assignments.

Are you ready to be a
Social Detective?

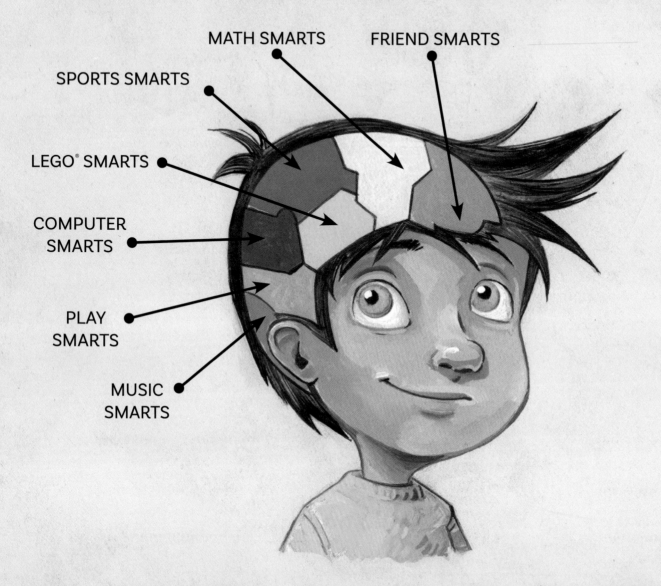

MATH SMARTS

FRIEND SMARTS

SPORTS SMARTS

LEGO® SMARTS

COMPUTER SMARTS

PLAY SMARTS

MUSIC SMARTS

In our brains there are all types of **"smarts."**
Some people have really great computer smarts,
music smarts, sports smarts, math smarts,
or even LEGO® smarts! What are your smarts?

Everyone knows that we use **school smarts** at school, but did you know we use our **social smarts** too?

SCHOOL SMARTS ●————→ ←————● SOCIAL SMARTS

Our **social smarts** help us figure out what is going on around us!

3

We use our **social smarts** whenever
we are around other people.

SOCIAL SMARTS

SOCIAL SMARTS

SOCIAL SMARTS

4

We use our **social smarts** to understand that
we notice and have **thoughts** about what others
are saying or doing, and they have thoughts too.

We use our **social smarts** everywhere—
NOT just in the classroom.

6

Social Detectives use their **social smarts** to collect important **CLUES.**

How?

They have
a secret, special,
social magnifying glass
to figure out
the situation and
gather lots of other
social clues too.

Situation = Place + People + What's happening?

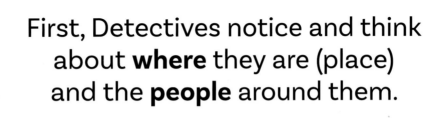

First, Detectives notice and think about **where** they are (place) and the **people** around them.

Then, they notice **what's happening** (action).

Let's try it.

Situation = _____ _____ _____

Place + People + What's happening?

Situation = _____ _____ _____

Place + People + What's happening?

11

Next, Social Detectives collect clues about the situation.

CLUE #1: Social Detectives use their **eyes** to notice the place, the people, what is happening, and what they may be planning to do next.

13

CLUE #2: Social Detectives use their **ears and eyes** to listen to what people are saying to figure out what's happening and what they plan to do next.

15

CLUE #4: Social Detectives also use their eyes, ears and brains to figure out how someone might be feeling.

This is all part of a Detective's **Smart Guess Toolbox.**

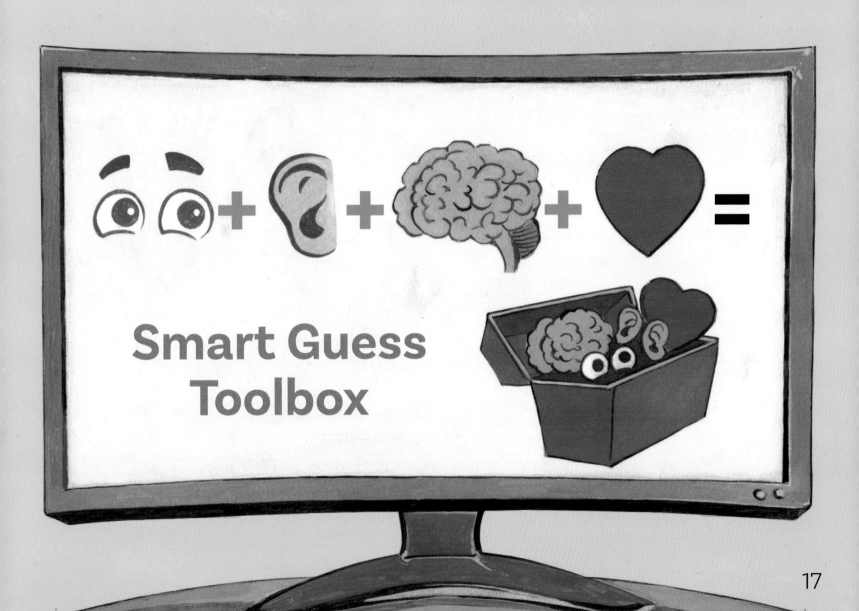

Smart Guess Toolbox

17

Let's practice making smart guesses!

Notice the clues to figure out:

Where is he?

What is happening?

What might he be thinking?

What might he be feeling?

What do you think he should do now/next?

Make a smart guess!

Where are they?

Who are the people?

What is happening?

What might they be thinking and feeling?

Can you figure out their plans?

19

Where are they?

Who are the people?

What's happening?

What is the group plan?

What might the people be feeling?

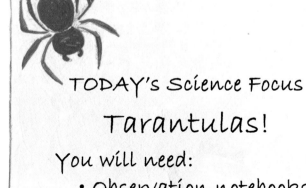

TODAY's Science Focus
Tarantulas!
You will need:
- Observation notebooks
- Critter chart
- Group work plan

We make **smart guesses**
all the time and everywhere we go.
We do this in class, on the playground,
with our families and in the community.

Others make smart guesses about us too.
They may think we are unfriendly
when we don't show interest in them.

22

Social Detectives gather more **CLUES**
to make smart guesses about the situation.

MY CLUES

- Look around.
- Think about the situation.
- Do I know these people or are they strangers?
- Listen to what others are saying.
- Think about what others are doing.

Reading

Volleyball

Four Square

Clue #5: Places can have many little situations.

There are three situations on the playground at recess.

24

CLUE #6:
Every SITUATION has a set of rules to help us figure out what to do or say.

Sometimes the RULES are written down or someone tells us and that makes it easier to figure out.

Other times the rules are **"hidden rules."**

MY CLUES

Even when some rules are written, there are still some parts that are hidden.

Hidden rules are the rules that people don't usually talk about out loud.

But we can make **smart guesses** to figure them out.

Hidden and written rules help us know the **expected behaviors** for that situation.

Let's look at the **LIBRARY** to see if we can figure out all of the rules— hidden and written.

26

Look at the three different library situations.
Can you find the written library rules?
Can you think of some hidden rules
(expected behaviors) for each situation?

27

CLUE #7: When people do or say what is **expected for the situation (Place + People + What's happening)**, others can have okay or calm thoughts and feelings.

FEELINGS

FEELINGS

28

When people feel okay or fine, their faces and bodies are calm, and their voices sound nice. They are also more relaxed.

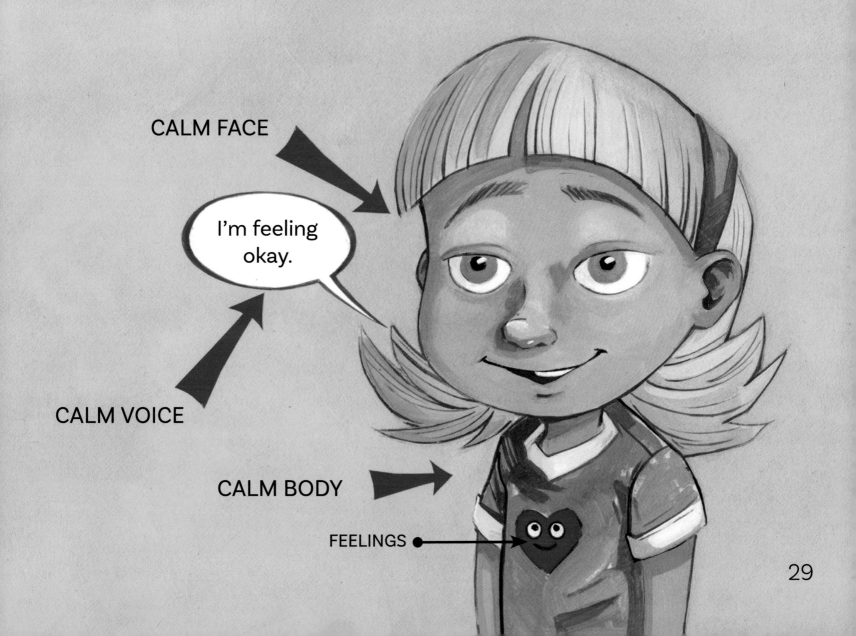

CALM FACE

I'm feeling okay.

CALM VOICE

CALM BODY

FEELINGS

When we are calm and relaxed, other people notice
and have calm (or okay) thoughts and feelings.
We all like being around others who feel calm because
being calm makes us feel fine or okay too.

Feelings Word Bank:

happy	calm
proud	good
excited	okay

Even moms and dads have okay or good thoughts and feelings when we use **expected behaviors** for the **situation**.

31

Let's practice looking for **hidden rules** to help us figure out expected behaviors for the situation!

32

It is an expected behavior to keep your **body in the group** when talking with others. This means keeping your body close to other people without touching them. Not too close and not too far away!

Look at the kids on the next page. They are ...

Thinking with their eyes

Keeping their bodies and brains in the group

Following the group plan

These are all **expected behaviors** in the classroom during teaching time.

34

Everyone is feeling calm and okay!
How can we tell their **brains are in the group**?

Use your Detective magnifying glass to figure out the situation (**Place** + **People** + **What's happening**), and what each person might be thinking and feeling.

Sometimes people do or say something **unexpected for the situation**.

Uh oh ...

38

CLUE #8: When people do or say what is **unexpected for the situation (Place + People + What's happening)** others can have **confused thoughts and feelings**.

Feelings Word Bank:

confused
angry
frustrated
sad
upset
annoyed
disappointed
unhappy
irritated

When we don't feel calm or okay, we may not seem friendly. We may use a mean-sounding voice or show an annoyed face. Our body gets tight. This means we are unhappy.

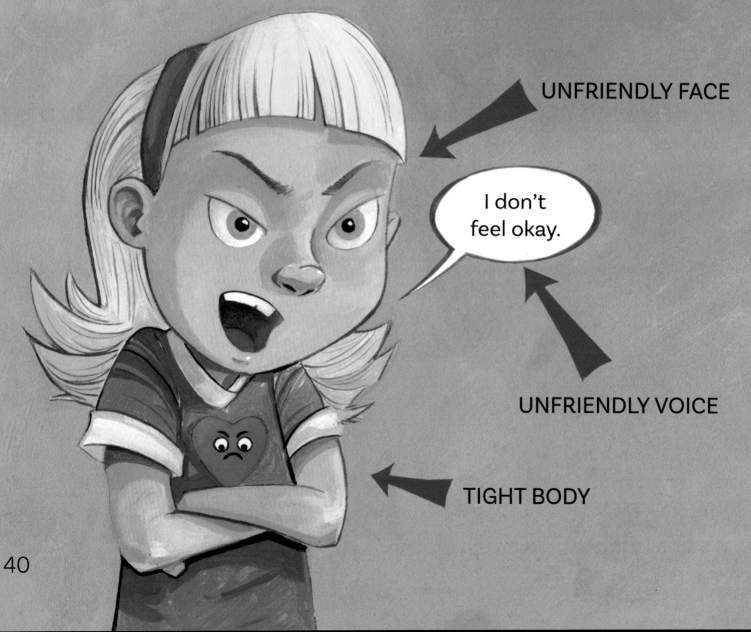

UNFRIENDLY FACE

I don't feel okay.

UNFRIENDLY VOICE

TIGHT BODY

When we don't feel okay or calm, we may not seem friendly. Other people notice and may have confused thoughts about our behavior. Most of us don't like being around others who are always upset because their feelings can make us have mad or upset feelings too.

Even dads, moms, grandmas, sisters and brothers can have **confused thoughts and feelings** if we do or say something unexpected for the situation.

42

43

Oh no! Whose **bodies and brains are not in the group?**
Who is not following the **group plan?**
Who is not **thinking with their eyes?**
These are all **unexpected behaviors** in the
classroom during teaching time. The teacher is
having angry thoughts and frustrated feelings!

What **unexpected behaviors** do you see for lining up to leave the classroom? Make a smart guess about the kids' thoughts and feelings.

45

Now we are ready to put everything together. But first let's review what we know (because we have learned a lot)!

46

Let's review!

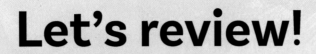

We all have **social smarts**.
Social Detectives collect lots of
clues to make **Smart Guesses**.

They figure out:

- The **Situation** = Place + People + What's happening?
- The **Hidden Rules** to know what behaviors are **expected** or **unexpected** for that situation
- How **behaviors** and **thoughts and feelings** are connected
- How a person's expected or unexpected **behaviors can affect how others feel** about the behavior

Now let's go practice!

Situation: Classroom + teacher/students + math lesson

Do you see **expected** or **unexpected** behaviors? Make smart guesses about how the teacher may be thinking and feeling.

What behaviors do you see that are **expected** or **unexpected** for this situation? What might the students be thinking or feeling?

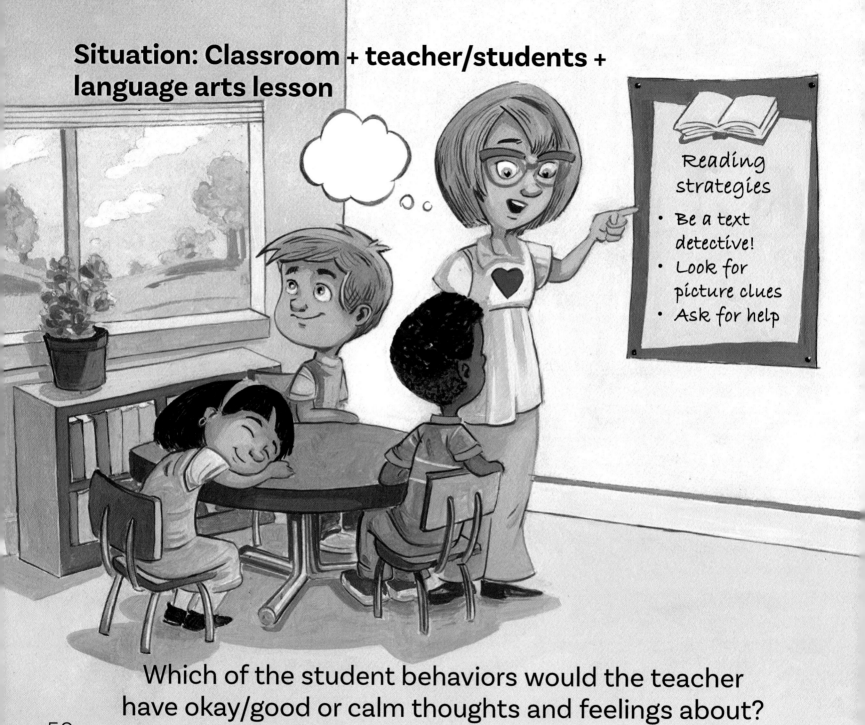

Which of the student behaviors would the teacher have okay/good or calm thoughts and feelings about?

What is Jake doing and saying?
Is it **expected** or **unexpected** for the situation?
What might his dad be thinking and feeling?

51

Hooray! You have started to grow your **SOCIAL SMARTS** as a Social Detective.

Now you are ready
to go to the
Superflex Academy!

53

Support and Extend the Learning

For more lessons and materials for interventionists (parents, caregivers, teachers, counselors, therapists) that help teach the concepts and vocabulary found in this book, refer to these materials:

The Superflex® Series for social learners starts here:

Book 1

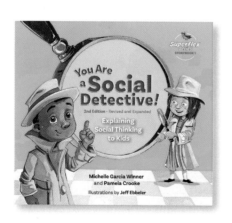

Book 2

More storybooks, visual supports, tools, and games in the Superflex series!

Stickers

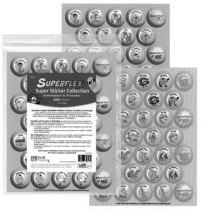

Posters

Games

Music

Books

Read hundreds of free articles on our website, including:
- *Superflex® Teaches Super Metacognitive Strategies*
- *10 DOs and DON'Ts for Teaching Superflex*

Check out our On Demand Series on Superflex:
- *Social Detective, Superflex®, and Friends Take On Social Emotional Learning: Teaching the Concepts with Fidelity*

To learn more, visit www.socialthinking.com.

SocialThinking has so much to offer!

OUR MISSION

Our mission is to help people develop social competencies to better connect with others and experience deeper well-being. We create unique teaching frameworks and strategies to help individuals develop their social thinking and social emotional learning to meet their academic, personal, and professional social goals. These goals often include sharing space effectively with others, learning to work as part of a team, and developing relationships of all kinds: with family, friends, classmates, co-workers, romantic partners, etc.

FREE ARTICLES & WEBINARS

100+ free educational articles and webinars about our teaching strategies

LIVESTREAM EVENTS, ON DEMAND COURSES & CUSTOM TRAINING

Live and recorded trainings for schools and organizations

PRODUCTS

Print and ebooks, games, decks, posters, music and more!

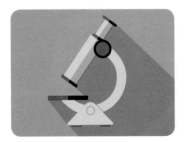

CLINICAL RESEARCH

Measuring the effectiveness of the Social Thinking® Methodology

SERVICES: CHILDREN & ADULTS

Clinical services, assessments, school consultations, etc.

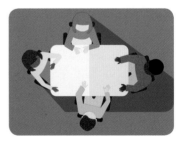

CLINICAL TRAINING PROGRAM

Three-day intensive training for professionals

www.socialthinking.com

About the Authors

Michelle Garcia Winner, MA, CCC-SLP, is the founder and CEO of Social Thinking and a globally recognized thought leader, author, speaker, and social-cognitive therapist. She is dedicated to helping people of all ages develop social emotional learning, including those with social learning differences. Across her 35+ year career she has created numerous evidence-based and evidence informed-strategies and teaching frameworks. Michelle's work also teaches how social competencies impact overall well-being, including one's ability to foster relationships and their academic and career performance. She and her team continually update the Social Thinking® Methodology based on the latest research and insights they learn from their clients. She was honored to receive a *Congressional Special Recognition Award* in 2008, and a *Lectureship Award* (2019) from the Society of Developmental and Behavioral Pediatricians.

Pamela Crooke, PhD, CCC-SLP, is the Chief Curriculum Officer and Director of Research, Content, Clinical Services, and the Social Thinking Training & Speakers' Collaborative. She served as a clinical faculty member of three universities and worked as a speech-language pathologist in the Arizona public schools for 15 years. Pam is a prolific speaker both in North America and abroad, has co-authored, with Michelle Garcia Winner, five award-winning books related to Social Thinking. Their book, *You Are a Social Detective!* 2nd Edition (2020), won the 2021 Creative Child Magazine Preferred Choice Award, the 2021 Mom's Choice Gold Medal Award, the 2021 Best Book Awards Finalist, and the 2022 International Book Awards Finalist. She and Winner collaborate on writing articles and blogs that appear on the Social Thinking website and in a wide array of publications. Her current research focuses on using practice-based research to examine how professionals and caregivers use frameworks and strategies within the Social Thinking® Methodology.

About the Illustrator

Jeffrey Ebbeler has been creating award winning art for children for over a decade. He has illustrated more than 40 picture books.